Kingdom Mind Shifts

Realigning our minds with the Gospels of Jesus

By James A Lilly

Contents

Recommendations

Mind shifts are never easy. Most often we feel much more comfortable with the status quo than opening our minds to something new and different. In *Kingdom Mind Shifts*, Jim Lilly has been willing to look beyond the status quo and ask challenging questions; questions that we all should be committed to think deeply about. You may not agree with all the conclusions that Jim will suggest, but you would do well to take the bold steps of asking yourself these questions and searching the scriptures for the answers. This is a short book, but it is packed with scriptural references that will help you in your search for answers to greater ministry fruitfulness.

This book contributes to the process of searching for clear Biblical injunctions as to how the church should function and particularly how to make disciples who make disciples as Jesus told us to do. He is a disciple-making practitioner who has served and continues to serve in many places around the world. What he shares in this little book comes from years of engagement with the scriptures and service on the field. Open your mind and heart and allow God to bring those mind shifts that will open you up to increased fruitfulness of ministry that you have never thought possible.

I pray that God will use this book for his glory.

Dave Hunt, VP New Generations (retired)

This little booklet By Jim Lilly, *Kingdom Mind Shifts,* takes you into a deep dive into the real understanding of discipleship. There are thousands of evangelists all over the world who make "converts", which makes them Pew sitters. The challenge before the church is to make disciples who make disciples. Otherwise, at best, the church will grow but fail to multiply. If the church has been commanded to reach the ends of the earth, then multiplying discipleship must remain its focus. Jesus' goal was to mature his followers into fishers of men. This booklet very forcefully and aptly addresses that issue.

Dr. Victor Choudhrie, Movement Leader in India, Author of *Greet the Ecclesia that Meets in Your Home,*

In *Kingdom Mind Shifts*, Jim Lilly does what he does best. He asks questions that make us move outside the box of our traditional thinking and consider things from a biblical perspective only. If we have been following Jesus for a long time, we sometimes assume that our paradigms are biblical when they are only assumptions from Christian culture.

But Jim does not do this to make us uncomfortable (although it does) or to merely cause us to change our strategies (although it will do that also). He does this because, after almost 2,000 years since Pentecost, half of the global population still lives in Unreached People Groups. The paradigms of mission have not gotten the job done. And the job of bringing Jesus to all peoples must be done.

This book makes us think. But most importantly it should make us act.

David Parish, President, World Missions and Evangelism, Inc. www.worldmissionsevangelism.com

Jim Lilly has been a hard-working and fruitful servant of the Lord Jesus for many years. Yet this book is not a narrative about him or his skill but is inspired by the Holy Spirit. It is written in simple language, so that broken-hearted sinners can connect directly with the biblical message of peace, reconciliation, and redemption of God, through Jesus Christ our Lord. Jim has faithfully complied with Peter's admonition, "But in your hearts honor Christ the Lord as holy, always being prepared to make a defense to anyone who asks you for a reason for the hope that is in you; get do it with gentleness and respect." 1 Peter 3:15

Pastor Ángel L. Montañez, Hijos Rey de Gloria Church, North Minneapolis, MN'

Jim Lilly is a disciple-maker. He has traveled globally, exploring some of today's many Disciple Making Movements. *Kingdom Mind Shifts* is a helpful attempt, especially for us in the West, to question some of the conclusions we have made concerning some of the Bible's great words and its Great Commission, so that we may find our lives and evangelistic efforts much more fruitful and enduring. I am sure that any Christian who "takes the bait" and answers the questions he poses, will be both challenged and blessed by the exercise, as I have been.

Dr. Edward N Gross, Compassion for Life International, Author of many books including, *Are You a Christian or a Disciple?*

"There is a saying among those who work to see Disciple-Making Movements; "You cannot give away what you don't possess." Jim Lilly is not writing about something he has not practiced himself and seen its success. He has been making disciples and training others to do the same for the last 11 years. *Kingdom Mind Shifts* will challenge paradigms you have held as almost sacred for years. If you have a heart for the lost, *Kingdom Mind Shifts* is a must-read.

Richard Williams, President of Compassion for Life International

Foreword

Recently I was reading a Christian magazine that discussed mobilizing the Church for missions. I read these types of articles to get fresh ideas for completing the Great Commission. However, the articles in this edition were trying to fulfill the Great Commission using a process based on an understanding that has not worked since the Church abandoned the model of St. Patrick.

If your understanding is incorrect, none of your solutions to your problem will work. What is your goal for the gospel, your church, and your lives? If you join us in the short book, we will look at our assumptions and understanding in light of the words of Jesus. Jesus is the way, the truth, and the life. How does what we do line up with what he told us and what he did?

Chapter 1
Reality of the Great Commission

Look, I tell you, lift up your eyes, and see that the fields are white for harvest. John 4:35b

One of Jesus' tools was to ask questions. Questions are powerful tools for change and improvement. The main point of this book is to challenge you to examine your own concepts and understandings and compare them to the Bible.

When we look at the traditional Church around the world and compare what happens there with the Book of Acts, we see very different results. The difference is illustrated below.

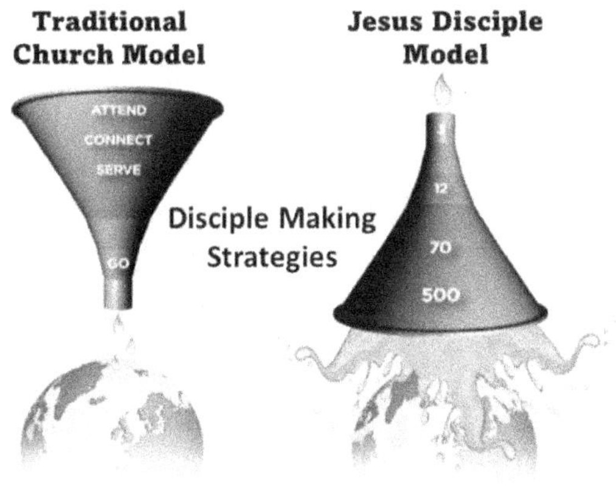

Used with permission of emotionallyhealthydiscipleship.org

If you have not considered these two realities before, take some time to reflect on them. What are the differences in outcomes when comparing the Acts of the Apostles with modern-day discipleship and traditional churches? Are they caused by not trying hard enough? Or because we are not doing the right things? Or because our understanding of what we are to do is not correct? Or are there other issues and reasons?

When we look at the traditional Church anywhere in the world, is it growing or is it shrinking? To answer my own question, all traditional denominations are seeing a loss of membership. Some individual churches are growing and expanding. Are they growing by reaching non-believers or are they growing by attracting members from other churches or fallen-away Christians?

The number of Christians in Europe has declined by 90% since the end of World War II. Europe is now the least-reached continent on the earth in terms of the total number of believers. Membership of churches in the US has declined more than 10% in the past 10 years and is projected to decline by more than 30% in the next generation. The Church in Egypt in 1870 was in one estimate, at about 70% of the population. It is now less than 10%. In Pakistan, the population of Christians was 3.4% in 1970. In 2020 it was 1.7%. Wherever you look in the world the traditional Church is contracting.

Is the model used by the traditional Church working well? Will doing more of the same improve the situation?

When I talk to people involved in traditional missions and ministries I rarely, if ever, hear them reflect upon their understanding of basic Christian truths. They talk about motivating the Church to do more. They discuss different strategies and approaches to reaching people and motivating people to serve. If this were the solution to the problem, we would have already had examples of great advances in the growth of the traditional Church.

To move us into a Biblical context, let us look at the first ten verses of the 19th chapter of the Acts of the Apostles. In this story, Apollos is in Corinth and Paul has gone to Ephesus. There he finds about twelve disciples. It turns out that they are disciples of John the Baptist and have been baptized with his baptism. Paul explains John's role was to prepare the way for Jesus. They accept this and are baptized in Jesus' name. Paul lays hands on them and they begin to speak in tongues and prophesy.

With these rebaptized and Spirit-filled disciples, he went to the synagogue, where he spoke boldly and reasoned with them to persuade them that the kingdom of God was at hand. After about three months some of the members became stubborn and resistant, speaking evil of "the Way" before the congregation.

Paul and his disciples leave the synagogue and go to the hall of Tyrannus where Paul speaks daily for the next two years. The result is that all of Asia hears the Word of the Lord, both Jew and Greek.

Before Paul challenged them, the twelve were not making an impact on their country. Afterward, the kingdom of God advances throughout their nation. Without delving into the particulars, we can say their understanding, though not wrong, was challenged and expanded.

Can you put the traditional Church and yourself in the place of the twelve disciples of John? The understanding is not wrong, but is something missing? I think so. The result is what we have in the illustration of the restrictive funnel. Let us imagine the understanding that you and these leaders have is challenged, and all receive a new empowerment. Is it possible that in two years all the area around each of you, millions of people, hear the Word of God? Is anything like this happening somewhere? The answer, is yes, around the world with church-planting and disciple-making movements, millions of people are being transformed by the knowledge of Jesus.

With this as a background, I would like us to ask nine questions about how our understanding aligns with the scriptures and particularly the teachings of Jesus. So, start by looking at your own understanding of some key components of our faith:

1. What is the good news that Jesus brought us?
    a. Jesus is love.
    b. He saved us from our sins.
    c. Other – What is your answer?
2. What is the purpose of the Church?
    a. For worship and fellowship.
    b. To receive teaching.
    c. Other – What is your answer?
3. What is "saving grace"?
    a. The love of God.
    b. God's mercy and unmerited favor.
    c. Other – What is your answer?
4. Who is called to fulfill the Great Commission?
    a. All Christians
    b. Trained missionaries and evangelists
    c. Other – What is your answer?
5. What is a disciple?
    a. Every Christian
    b. The Twelve Apostles
    c. Other – What is your answer?
6. Is there a difference between a believer, a follower, and a disciple of Jesus?
    a. Yes
    b. No

7. What is the work of ministry that every saint is to be equipped to do?
   a. Faithfully attend and serve a church.
   b. Love God and Love people.
   c. Other – What is your answer?
8. Is there a difference between modern-day discipleship and disciple-making?
   a. Yes
   b. No
9. Considering what you understand about Jesus, what is your purpose and goal for your life?
   a. To love God and be faithful.
   b. To become more like Jesus.
   c. Other – What is your answer?

Let us begin by examining these nine questions a little deeper. First, our understanding of the good news of Jesus forms the understanding and purpose of our lives. People who do not know Jesus live their lives in significantly different ways than those who do. If our understanding of the good news is not what Jesus said it is, will our lives and efforts operate with his power?

Second, the understanding of the purpose of the church directs much of the efforts of Christians. Are we investing our time and effort most effectively? What we are doing may look right, but is it achieving the purposes that Jesus intended?

Next, what is saving grace? Does our understanding align with the gospels? "We are saved by grace through faith," writes Paul, but if our understanding of grace does not align with that of Jesus, what does that mean?

Fifth, what is a disciple? Can you identify unique practices of a disciple that make their life different than those who believed in Jesus because of the miracles he performed?

Who is called to fulfill the Great Commission? All Christians? All Believers? All followers? All disciples? Are these terms interchangeable? What is a disciple?

Seventh, Ephesians 4:11-12 instructs all positions of authority and leadership to equip the saints for the work of ministry. How are they to be equipped? What is the ministry they are to be equipped to do?

Eighth, we all probably have an idea of discipling someone. What are the good aspects of discipling someone? Are there bad or limiting aspects? Would it be better to be a disciple of Jesus? Is it possible to be discipled by Jesus today? How might you distinguish between discipling someone and disciple-making with Jesus?

Finally, our understanding of Jesus and what he calls us to personally, sets the stage and determines the limits of how we see and respond to his offer and how we live our lives. What was his call to his disciples? What did they do after he returned to heaven? What needed to happen before they were able to do it?

If our understanding of these nine questions does not align with the understanding of Jesus and his disciples, is it possible that a significant part of the decline in the Church may be attributed to us and our understandings and expectations?

Fortunately, not all the news of the Church is about decline. In China, the Church has grown from a few million to 70 to 120 million people since 1970. In India, the number of new believers, followers, and disciples of Jesus has increased about three-fold, to between 50 and 70 million since 1990. As of 2010, Asia has as many as, or more Christians than North or South America. Africa likewise has more than either of either of the Americas though less than Asia. Is the understanding of these growing churches different than that of the traditional Church?

Today, in these rapidly multiplying churches we have many opportunities to see people coming into a relationship with Jesus similar to that testified to in the Acts of the Apostles. That means that we can compare our understanding both with the Bible and with living people who are seeing thousands of people come to know Jesus Christ and are fulfilling the Great Commission.

Before moving on to looking at the gospels, take some time to consider the nine questions once again. What are your answers? Most people reading this book will have strongly held opinions about some of them. For others, you will not have thought about them deeply.

Chapter 2
Examining the Scriptures

Then he opened their minds to understand the Scriptures, Luke 24:45

As you look at the following scripture passages, ask God for understanding and compare this with your current understanding to see if there are differences. Then consider what that means to your own life and the mission of the Church. It will be helpful to discuss each of these with one or two friends. It will also be good to have a Bible available as you read.

1. **What is the good news (gospel) of Jesus**? How does this differ from your own understanding? If there is a difference, what should change in what you do to serve God?

Look at Matthew 4:23, Matthew 9:35; Matthew 24:14; Mark 1:15; Luke 8:1; Luke 16:16; and Acts 8:12

Matthew 4:23 *he went throughout all Galilee, teaching in their synagogues and proclaiming the gospel of the kingdom and healing every disease and every affliction among the people.*

Matthew 9:35 *Jesus went throughout all the cities and villages, teaching in their synagogues and proclaiming the gospel of the kingdom, and healing every disease and every affliction.*

Matthew 24:14 *And this gospel of the kingdom will be proclaimed throughout the whole world as a testimony to all nations, and then the end will come.*

2. **What is the purpose of the Church?** (Following are the two times Jesus mentions the church in the four gospels.) How would this be lived out by the church? How does this compare with your understanding of its purpose? What are the two expectations that Jesus has for his church? How are these lived out in your church? Are they priorities?

Look at Matthew 16:13-19 and Matthew 18:17

Matthew 16:18b *I will build my church, and the gates of hell shall not prevail against it.*

Matthew 18:17a *If he refuses to listen to them, tell it to the church. And if he refuses to listen even to the church, . . .*

3. **What is "saving grace"?** This will take some reflection on both your experience and understanding. At what point or in what position in his relationship with God is a person saved? What are the conditions at that moment? What took place to make it happen? Now, look at the following passage and identify those points.

John 14:15-23

"If you love me, you will keep my commandments. [16] And I will ask the Father, and he will give you another Helper, to be with you forever, [17] even the Spirit of truth, whom the world cannot receive, because it neither sees him nor knows him. You know him, for he dwells with you and will be in you. . . .. [23] Jesus answered him, "If anyone loves me, he will keep my word, and my Father will love him, and we will come to him and make our home with him.

4. **Who is called to fulfill the Great Commission?** What does it take to meet this requirement? The search for the answer to this leads to question five.

Matthew 28:16ff
Now the eleven disciples went to Galilee, to the mountain to which Jesus had directed them.

5. What is a disciple?

If you do not know what a disciple is or what is expected, you will not be successful in making one. Since disciples make disciples, to make one you must be one.

There is a results-oriented proof in John 15:8, '*that you glorify God the Father, by bearing much fruit and so prove to be my disciples*.' How is that done? The complete answer to how this is accomplished is not found in one place in the Bible. Dr. Ed Gross in his book "Are You a Christian or a Disciple?" provides some direction in his list of five practices of every first-century disciple of every rabbi. These five would have been common understanding to the disciples of Jesus. Discipling someone requires demonstration as well as instruction. In the following passages you can see Jesus demonstrating them and expecting his disciples to do the same:

I. Obeys his master's commands:
    Demonstration: John 10:17-18, Matthew 26:39. Philippians 2:8

John 17:17-18 *For this reason the Father loves me, because I lay down my life that I may take it up again. No one takes it from me, but I lay it down of my own accord. I have authority to lay it down, and I have authority to take it up again. This charge I have received from my Father.*
Matthew 26:39 *And going a little farther he fell on his face and prayed, saying, "My Father, if it be possible, let this cup pass from me; nevertheless, not as I will, but as you will."*
Philippians 2:8 *And being found in human form, he humbled himself by becoming obedient to the point of death, even death on a cross.*

Expectation: John 14:15; John 20:21

John 14:15 *If you love me, you will keep [obey] my commandments.*

John 20:21 *Jesus said to them again, "Peace be with you. As the Father has sent me, even so, I am sending you.*

II.   <u>Memorizes his master's teaching to teach others</u>:
Demonstration: John 14:24

John 14:24 *And the word that you hear is not mine but the Father's who sent me.*

Expectation: John 8:31; 15:7; Matthew 24:14

John 18:31 *So Jesus said to the Jews who had believed him, "If you abide in my word, you are truly my disciples,*

John 15:7 *If you abide in me, and my words abide in you, ask whatever you wish, and it will be done for you.*

Matthew 24:14 *And this gospel of the kingdom will be proclaimed throughout the whole world as a testimony to all nations, and then the end will come.*

III.   <u>Knows the Old Testament and what his Master taught about it</u>:
Demonstration: Matthew 5:17ff; John 14:24

Matthew 5:17 *Do not think that I have come to abolish the Law or the Prophets; I have not come to abolish them but to fulfill them. [18] For truly, I say to you, until heaven and earth pass away, not an iota, not a dot, will pass from the Law until all is accomplished.*

Matthew 5:21-22 *You have heard that it was said to those of old, 'You shall not murder; and whoever murders will be liable to judgment. [22] But I say to you that everyone who is angry with his brother will be liable to judgment; whoever insults his brother will be liable to the council; and whoever says, 'You fool!' will be liable to the hell of fire.*

John 14:24 *Whoever does not love me does not keep my words. And the word that you hear is not mine but the Father's who sent me.*

Expectation: Matthew 13:52

And he said to them, "Therefore every scribe who has been trained for the kingdom of heaven is like a master of a house, who brings out of his treasure what is new and what is old."

IV.   <u>Imitates his master, both his actions and mission</u>:
Demonstration: John 5:19; John 10:37

John 5:19 *Jesus said to them, "Truly, truly, I say to you, the Son can do nothing of his own accord, but only what he sees the Father doing. For whatever the Father does, that the Son does likewise.*

John 10:37 *If I am not doing the works of my Father, then do not believe me.*

Expectation: John 13:15-16

For I have given you an example, that you also should do just as I have done to you. [16] Truly, truly, I say to you, a servant is not greater than his master, nor is a messenger greater than the one who sent him.

V.   <u>Makes disciples using their rabbi's teachings</u>:
Demonstration: Throughout the four gospels, e.g., John 8:31; Luke 6:12-13

John 8:31 *So, Jesus said to the Jews who had believed him, "If you abide in my word, you are truly my disciples,*

Luke 6:12-13 *In these days he went out to the mountain to pray, and all night he continued in prayer to God. And when day came, he called his disciples and chose from them twelve, whom he named apostles:*

Expectation: **Matthew 28:19**

Go therefore and [Having gone] make disciples of all nations, baptizing them in the name of the Father and of the Son and of the Holy Spirit, [edit from Greek].

Extra: The Unique Requirement of Jesus _ To hold Jesus as more precious than your own life. This one condition is beyond the expectation of the disciple of any other rabbi. Look at **Luke 14:25-27**.

[25] Now great crowds accompanied him, and he turned and said to them [26] "If anyone comes to me and does not hate his own father and mother and wife and children and brothers and sisters, yes, and even his own life, he cannot be my disciple. [27] Whoever does not bear his own cross and come after me cannot be my disciple.

In Romans 10:9 Paul referred to this when he said that confessing that Jesus is 'Lord' is a requirement for salvation.

If you compare your life to this list of practices of a typical disciple in the time of Jesus, what areas are you strong in, and in what areas could you grow as a disciple of Jesus?

6. **Is there a difference between a believer, a follower, and a disciple?**

To understand the importance of this question study Matthew 28:18 and 28:20 and consider the involvement and relationship of Jesus in making disciples. What is the involvement of Jesus and the relationship with his disciples as they make disciples?

Matthew 28:18 - 20

And Jesus came and said to them, "All authority in heaven and on earth has been given to me. . . [20] teaching them to observe [obey] all that I have commanded you. And behold, I am with you always, to the end of the age."

After looking at the interaction of Jesus and the disciples in making disciples of the nations, consider the differences between being a believer, a follower, and a disciple.

Believers: You know John 3:16, but also look at John 2:23-24 and Jesus' relationship with believers. Will Jesus entrust himself to them?

John 2:23-24 *Now when he was in Jerusalem at the Passover Feast, many believed in his name when they saw the signs that he was doing. *[24]* But Jesus on his part did not entrust himself to them, because he knew all people.*

Followers: Matthew 4:19 and then Luke 14:25-27, and 33

Matthew 4:19 - *And he said to them, "Follow me, and I will make you fishers of men."*

Luke 14:25-27; 33 (NLT) *A large crowd was following Jesus. He turned around and said to them, *[26]* "If you want to be my disciple, you must, by comparison, hate everyone else—your father and mother, wife and children, brothers, and sisters—yes, even your own life. Otherwise, you cannot be my disciple. *[27]* And if you do not carry your own cross and follow me, you cannot be my disciple. *[33]* So you cannot become my disciple without giving up everything you own.*

Disciple: Review the list of five-plus-one practices of a disciple in question 5, and in light of Luke 14 verses above, look at Matthew 28:16.

7. **What is the work of ministry that every saint is to be equipped to do and how is that done?**

In Ephesians 4:11-12, from the perspective of the apostles, prophets, evangelists, shepherds, and teachers being disciples of Jesus, how are they going to equip the saints and what are they going to equip them to do?

As was described earlier, to be a disciple is to look at things from the perspective of your rabbi. Look at everything Jesus did and then look at the partial list below.

Luke 19:9 *the Son of Man came to seek and to save the lost.*
John 3:16b *whoever believes in him should not perish but have eternal life.*
2 Corinthians 5:18-19 *All this is from God, who through Christ reconciled us to himself and gave us the ministry of reconciliation; [19] that is, in Christ God was reconciling the world to himself, not counting their trespasses against them, and entrusting to us the message of reconciliation.*
Matthew 28:19-20 (NLT) *Therefore, [having gone] make disciples of all the nations, baptizing them in the name of the Father and the Son and the Holy Spirit. [20] Teach these new disciples to obey all the commands I have given you. And be sure of this: I am with you always, even to the end of the age. [edit is from the Greek].*

8. **Is there a difference between traditional discipleship and disciple-making?** Is it possible to be discipled by Jesus? How would that be different than the traditional understanding of discipleship? What is the Biblical model for traditional discipleship?

   Begin by considering your understanding of modern discipleship. Then look at: John 14:18, Matthew 18:20, John 1:1, John 14:26, Matthew 23:8-11

John 14: 18 *I will not leave you as orphans; I will come to you.*
Matthew 18:20 *For where two or three are gathered in my name, there am I among them.*

John 1:1 *In the beginning was the Word, and the Word was with God, and the Word was God.*

John 14:26 *But the Helper, the Holy Spirit, whom the Father will send in my name, he will teach you all things and bring to your remembrance all that I have said to you.*

Matthew 23:8-11 *But you are not to be called rabbi, for you have one teacher, and you are all brothers. [9] And call no man your father on earth, for you have one Father, who is in heaven [10] Neither be called instructors, for you have one instructor, the Christ. [11] The greatest among you shall be your servant.*

9. Considering what you understand about Jesus, what is your purpose and goal for your life?

Look at: John 14:12, John 4:19, John 20:21-22; review Question 5, all the practices of a disciple. What is the focus of Jesus and his expectations of his disciples?

John 14:12 *"Truly, truly, I say to you, whoever believes in me will also do the works that I do; and greater works than these will he do, because I am going to the Father.*

John 4:19 *And he said to them, "Follow me, and I will make you fishers of men.*

John 20:21-22 *"Jesus said to them again, "Peace be with you. As the Father has sent me, even so I am sending you." [22] And when he had said this, he breathed on them and said to them, "Receive the Holy Spirit.*

How did your understanding line up with the passages have studied in the Bible? Are there some areas you need to adjust both your thinking and actions?

If you want to see how to put this new understanding into practice look at some of the 1950+ disciple-making and church-planting movements around the world. *"Miraculous*

Movements" by Jerry Trousdale and "*Bhojpuri Breakthrough*," by Victor Johns are two good books to start reading.

At this point, I hope you have begun to see that some key parts of your understanding need to be adjusted if it is to line up with the scripture. The misalignments that we have between our thinking and the Bible are a large contributor to the decline of the traditional Church. The exploding disciple-making and church-planting movements have a different understanding. They have shed many of the extra-Biblical understandings. They are growing exponentially throughout the world.

Once our thinking is in better alignment with the Bible, we then need to change what we do and increase our expectations.

Instead of our goal being to make believers in Jesus who attend church regularly, our goal needs to be to make disciples who will make more disciples and change the world. Instead of teaching and training doctrine, history, and protocols, we need to teach people how to hear from God in the Bible and be taught by the Holy Spirit.

A campus pastor of a mega-church recently shared with me his frustration with their training. After completing two and one-half years of their church's training, people could not even lead a small group. All their training was focused on improving their understanding of Biblical truth and learning to conform their lives to healthy Christian practices as laid out in the Epistles. But they were not "equipped for the work of the ministry."

As Paul and the author of Hebrews wrote, instead of feeding the people in our church "milk," we need to equip them to be able to feed themselves on the solid meat of the scriptures. Becoming disciples of Jesus by learning to obediently apply the words of scripture to their lives is an important aspect of what it means to equip the saints.

Chapter 3

My Understanding of the Nine Questions

*For now we see in a mirror dimly, but then face to face.
Now I know in part; then I shall know fully, even as I
have been fully known. – 1 Corinthians 13:12*

As I offer my opinions and experiences, the goal is not that
you agree with everything I write, but that they would give
you another perspective to consider. As Paul wrote in the
Corinthians passage above and Jesus said, when he spoke of
the tribulation, we humans only know and see in part. The
point of this book is that you start searching the Bible and
realign both your understanding and your actions with it in
order to see the kingdom of heaven advance upon the earth. If
our understanding is misaligned, then our objectives and goals
will be misaligned, and our efforts will bear little fruit.

1.   What is the good news of Jesus?

This is one of my favorite questions to ask people. Their
answer is usually a good indication of how they are living
their lives. The very nominal Christian may answer, "Jesus is
love. He came so we can love one another." The typical
evangelical answer is something like: "We were separated
from God because of our sins. Jesus came to pay the penalty
for our sin, so our relationship with God is restored and we
can go to heaven." But Jesus said his good news was that the
kingdom of God or the kingdom of heaven was among us. Is
there a substantial difference between the gospel of
reconciliation and the gospel of the kingdom? I believe there

is. If the good news of Jesus stops at reconciliation with God and the promise of going to heaven, then there is nothing left for us to do on earth.

A friend of mine told me the story of his daughter's four-year-old son. This child came to his mother one day and said, "I want to die and go and be with Jesus." She was alarmed and told him, "Jesus wants us to tell other people about him before we die." He nodded and went away. A few days later, he came back to his mother and said, "I told the neighbor girl about Jesus and prayed with her. Now can I die and go to heaven to be with Jesus?"

Most of us have heard similar stories or remarks from different people, often adults, from time to time. Bringing the kingdom of God to earth gives everyone a mission for their lives. The gospel of reconciliation alone does not.

So, where does "reconciliation" fit in? If we look at the first four lines of the Lord's prayer in Matthew 6, I believe Jesus lays out a full gospel orientation:

> *"Our Father in heaven,*
> *Hallowed be your name.*
> *Your kingdom come,*
> *Your will be done, on earth as it is in heaven.*

"Our Father in heaven" – this is the reconciliation part of the gospel. Without it, there is nothing of value, for out of this relationship of love everything that has life flows. So, the evangelical "gospel" is very much a critical part of the good news, but it is not all of it.

"Hallowed be your name" – How do we best glorify the Father? Should we do it the way that Jesus did? To imitate his example fully is to become his disciple. When Jesus sent his disciples to make disciples, this was what he was calling them to do.

"Your kingdom come" – This is the mission part of the Good News of Jesus. In Luke 17:20 and 21, Jesus was asked when the kingdom of God would come. 'He said it is not coming in ways that can be observed, "Behold, the kingdom is among you."' Wherever people live under the kingship of Jesus, God's kingdom is there. A kingdom is simply a group of families and people who live under and in obedience to a king. They have a culture consistent with the king's commands and laws.

"Your will be done" – Notice that Luke's version does not contain this line. I believe that God's will being done is evidence of his kingdom's reign upon the earth, not something we seek to do directly.

There is the story of the Welsch Revival of the early 20th Century when the constables wore white gloves because there was no crime in Wales. There is a similar story during the Guatemalan Revival of the 1980s when the sheriff did not lock the jail, because there was no crime in that region. Then there is a more recent story in Cuba.

I asked a movement leader in that country if he was experiencing persecution from the Communist government. He laughed and said that within that month he had been visited by chief constables of two different cities. They both said about the same thing: "Do you know that we know what you have been doing? What do you think that Havana would do if they found out? But don't stop, they each said, the crime rate in our city has dropped more than 90%." He told me with a smile, that the most productive church planters in those cities were former gang leaders who had come to Jesus. – When God's kingdom comes his will IS done.

A personal observation, demonstrating the love of God in action, is part of introducing the kingdom, but if you try to do God's will without establishing his kingdom, you will be in for a lifetime of frustration.

2.   What is the purpose of the Church?

Jesus only mentioned the church twice in the gospels. He gives two purposes. In Matthew 16 he says that upon the bedrock as demonstrated by Peter, he will build his church and the gates of hell will not stand against it.

As I look at this passage, I see a little play on words. When Jesus calls Simon, Peter (Petros) the word means a rock or stone. Then he says upon this (Petra) he will build his church. Petra means bedrock. If you picture Jesus talking to Simon when he names him Petros and then picture him extending his arms to take in all the disciples when he says, upon this bedrock, Petra, I will build my church, you could understand Jesus to emphasize that his church would be built upon the bedrock of disciples. Hence equipping the saints for the work of the ministry in Ephesians 4:12, by making disciples would conform to this understanding of Jesus' comment and align it with Jesus' final command to make disciples of all nations.

The first mission of the church Jesus gave was that it would successfully attack the gates of hell. What does the expression, "the gates of hell" mean? I have in my mind Colossians 1:13 where we are delivered from the dominion of darkness into the kingdom of his beloved son. The church is to be externally focused on gaining territory for God's reign upon the earth.

How are they to be attacked? Matthew 28:18 commands the disciples to make disciples of all nations. Acts 1:8 says we are to start in our hometown, then our country, then our neighboring country, and then to the ends of the earth.

Matthew 24:14 says the good news of the kingdom is to be proclaimed in all the world.

The second mission of the church as outlined in Matthew 18 is to govern conflicts and be the final arbiter of disputes.

These two purposes are in alignment with the common use of the word ecclesia (church) at the time of Jesus. The Ecclesia was the governing body of colonists that was established by an "apostle" under the authority of the conquering Roman empire. The duty of the ecclesia was to establish and extend the culture, authority, and government of the king or emperor into the subjugated country. (Matthew 6:10) We know that that king is the Lord and his Christ (Revelations 11:15).

Certainly, there are other things the church can do, but Jesus gave these two. As you look at your church, how are these two incorporated into your church's purpose, activities, and mission? As you think of the two funnels in Chapter 1, could their presence or absence be correlated to the church's success or failure in bringing the good news to your community?

3.   What is "saving" grace?

Is there any other term more used among Christians than the word grace? Is the best definition of grace, "the unmerited favor of God?" Is it, "our gain at Christ's expense?"

Dietrich Bonhoeffer spoke of "cheap grace' as a concept of grace that is watered down to the point it has no substance. In the second chapter of Ephesians, Paul says twice that we are saved by grace and once that it is a gift of God and not by our own doings. What is this grace that saves us? Some people and churches teach that because of the grace given us through Jesus, all are saved; no one is in danger of going to hell. There are all different shades of understanding, but where is a Biblical definition of Grace? NT Wright in a lecture, said that everyone needs to have a Biblical basis for their understanding of Grace. His was found in John 14:21-23.

It was while I was part of our first mission agency that the importance of understanding grace was made clear to me. I had just been introduced to disciple-making and was teaching a class at the Bible school affiliated with that mission agency. I taught on John 14:15-26. The head of the mission agency took issue that I read John 14:15 which says, "If you love me, you will obey my commandments." He said, "Don't you believe that we are saved by grace?" I said, "Yes, but Jesus said that to love him means we will obey him." Then he quoted Ephesians 2:8 and 9, *"For by grace you have been saved through faith. And this is not your own doing; it is the gift of God, not a result of works, so that no one may boast."* When I again pointed to Jesus's words, he said, "Don't you believe Paul had further revelation beyond that of Jesus?"

As I thought about this encounter, I realized that I had never seriously looked at what grace was; how it worked; or what it really meant. Is it possible that "grace" negates the commands of Jesus? So, I began to look at the scriptures and what they said.

I started with Romans 10:9, "If you confess with your lips that Jesus is Lord and believe in your heart that God raised him from the dead, you will be saved." I had used this passage in my days as a street evangelist. At that time, I had understood it to say that if a person says that Jesus is Lord and believes that God raised him from the dead he would be saved. I would have people affirm or pray this in their prayer to receive Jesus.

However, if you look at the words, it says, "If you **confess** with your lips that Jesus is **Lord,** as well as believe in you heart that God raised him from the dead you will be saved." (My emphasis) Is there a difference between confessing something and saying something? Confessions are testimony of a reality you are living out. If you confess a crime, you are guilty of it. Profession or saying something you want or believe to be true is not the same as confession. Effectively, the passage is saying, are you guilty of having Jesus as your Lord? Are you guilty of obeying him in everything?

Matthew in the 26th chapter of his gospel has an interesting dialogue between Jesus and his disciples at their final meal together:

*And as they were eating, he said, "Truly, I say to you, one of you will betray me." 22 And they were very sorrowful and began to say to him one after another, "Is it I, **Lord**?" 23 He answered, "He who has dipped his hand in the dish with me will betray me. 24 The Son of Man goes as it is written of him, but woe to that man by whom the Son of Man is betrayed! It would have been better for that man if he had not been born." 25 Judas, who would betray him, answered, "Is it I, **Rabbi [Teacher]**?" He said to him, "You have said so." [My emphasis.]*

Matthew is making a very subtle distinction here between "Lord" and "Teacher," which has great implications.

Your Lord is someone you obey and are willing to give your life for. If he gives an order, you do it. Is that what we understand when we say that Jesus is Lord? Paul, in Romans 10:9, is saying in other words, that the person who lives a life of obedience to Jesus and believes God raised him from the dead, will be saved. In Ephesians 2, he also said that we are saved by grace, through faith, not through our efforts. So, what was Paul's understanding of grace and salvation?

Looking at the gospels, we find that Jesus never uses the word grace. In the first chapter of John's gospel, John says that

Jesus is full of grace. We find that through him, we all receive grace upon grace, and that grace and truth came through him. But what is grace? Since he is full of grace and the source of grace, then when we look at Jesus and his life, we should be able to discover grace.

In John 14:15 through 17 Jesus says, "If you love me, you will obey my commandments." Then Jesus says he would ask the Father to send us the Spirit of truth. This Spirit had been <u>with</u> the disciples, but in the future, it would be <u>in</u> them. When the Spirit of truth is in us, what is our relationship with God? Is this connected to saving-grace? Is it a gift?

In Acts 10 and again in Acts 15, Peter makes note of God sending his Holy Spirit as a sign of full acceptance into the kingdom of heaven.

Acts 15:8 And God, who knows the heart, bore witness to them, by giving them the Holy Spirit *just as he did to us, [9] and he made no distinction between us and them, having cleansed their hearts by* faith.

In John 14:21, Jesus says whoever has his commands and keeps them loves him. Jesus will then manifest himself to that person. What is that person's relationship with Jesus at that moment? Is this connected to grace?

In John 14:23, Jesus says, that if anyone loves him, that person will keep or obey his word and the Father will love him and both the Father and Jesus will abide with him. If the Father, Jesus, and the Holy Spirit abide with us and are in us, are we saved? How is this related to "saving grace?"

NT Wright said his definition of grace is "the presence of God working in us." My definition is similar, **"Grace is the presence and power of God working in us and through us to accomplish his will for his glory."** (vs 23 and 16) It is hinged on two things, that we love Jesus and that we obey his commandments.

Is there a difference between obeying out of love or does this mean depending on our own works? The answer is obvious. We do our "work" with our own planning and initiative. Obedience means to respond to directions or commands. The obedience that Jesus and his Father are looking for flows out of our love for Him.

But what about John 3:16, that those who believe in Jesus will have eternal life? It seems that with eternal life comes a new relationship with God the Father. We are born anew. (John 3) As I pointed out at the beginning of this chapter, we see that reconciliation with God and acceptance as his sons and daughters is an essential component of the good news of Jesus.

We cannot continue the work of Jesus without a father-child relationship with God. The Father sent the Son. Through the Son's atoning work we are called "sons of the Father." (Matthew 5:45) The Son sends us (John 20:21) with his unfinished assignments. Jesus completed the essential task of reconciling us with the Father, but has left us the remaining work of bringing his kingdom to earth. The goal of becoming a disciple of Jesus is focused on completing this work. Reconciliation with the Father and becoming like Jesus are necessary, but the purpose is not our self-improvement or our holiness, but fulfilling God's purposes and glory.

If grace is the power and presence of God working in us and through us, then we should expect that he will accomplish things through us for his glory. This brings us to Jesus's final command. Jesus told us to make disciples, not just make converts or believers. The goal of making a convert is to have the person believe. The goal of making a disciple is to have them both love and obey Jesus. Out of this relationship, his disciples are to complete the work he left them.

4. Who is called to fulfill the Great Commission?

The answer is found in Matthew 28:16-20, The eleven disciples went, worshipped, doubted, were assured, and instructed. They had previously been trained and tested. Jesus was willing to make his authority available to them and to accompany them in the work he gave them of making disciples. He did not send a group of believers or even followers. He sent disciples.

To try to get people who are not disciples of Jesus to fulfill the Great Commission is an exercise that will continue to fail. The reason for this small book is to help us rethink and realign our efforts with the Bible. If we are **not** equipping the saints to become disciples of Jesus, we have missed the point of the Great Commission, which might better be called the Great Partnership. It has always been to make disciples. Only disciples can complete it.

5. What is a disciple?

In simplest terms, a disciple of Jesus did what Jesus did and what he said to do. Knowing what things to look for helps to identify them in the scriptures. The following five key practices provide tangible items that can be used to measure a person's progress in growing as a disciple; both your own and those you might coach.

While these are not specifically listed in the Bible, according to First-century discipleship scholars including Michael Wilkins, D. Thomas Lancaster, and Edward Gross, they were commonly assumed by all rabbis in the first century. Jesus himself modeled all of them and he called for them from his disciples.

Obey

In order of importance, *obeying his master's commands* is the first on the list. We see that Jesus modeled it in his life to 'seek and save the lost.' In John 15:10 he points out that he kept his father's commands out of love, and he expects his disciples to do the same. In John 10:17-19 we see that he clearly understood and was committed to obey his father's command to lay down his life for the sheep. Paul in Philippians 2 characterized Jesus's entire mission to the earth as a mission of obedience. Jesus in his final discourse to his disciples in John sends them just as he was sent, to do what he did. As he obeyed, we are to obey.

Know and Teach Jesus' Teachings

The second practice in this list, but the first item for a new disciple was to *commit his master's teaching to memory and to teach others*. A disciple obeyed what he learned as soon as he learned it. Obedience to what is learned leads to understanding.

Jesus demonstrated that he did this in that every word he said was the word that his Father gave him. In John 15:7 we see that Jesus expected his words to abide in each of his disciples. In Matthew 10 and Luke 10, disciples are instructed to proclaim the kingdom of heaven.

In the first verse of Matthew 5, we see that when Jesus saw the crowds of people he went up on the mountain, sat down and his disciples came to him, and he began to teach them. In the next to last verse of chapter 7 we learn that the crowds were astounded at his teachings. Did Jesus project his voice from a seated position to large crowds? What role did the disciples play in passing the teachings on to the crowds? The scripture does not say, but the description fits the model of

Jesus teaching the disciples, then the disciples would have taught the crowds.

Committing to memory and sharing what a disciple learns are imperatives for a disciple. You cannot obey what you do not know. You cannot tell others what you do not know. The Holy Spirit cannot bring to your remembrance what you have not stored there.

Know the Old Testament and Jesus' Teachings about it.

To have a solid understanding of the mission of Jesus, a disciple needs to know the Old Testament. He or she needs to understand the involvement of Jesus and the Spirit of God in the creation. They need to understand the origin of sin and the fall of man, as well as God's promise from the Garden of Eden to understand why and what Jesus did for us on the cross. They need to understand the prophecies and foreshadowing of Jesus throughout the Old Testament.

In addition to Jesus' teaching in Matthew 5 about the Old Testament, his entire life was a teaching on and fulfillment of the Old Testament.

In Matthew 13:52, Jesus described his expectation for his disciples saying that they would be scribes trained for the kingdom of heaven and be like masters of a house who would bring out both new and old treasures.

Imitates his master, both his actions and mission:

Jesus on numerous occasions referenced that his Father was working and therefore he was working. He also said he did what he saw his Father doing. Jesus perfectly imitated the Father.

When Jesus washed his disciples' feet in John 13, he did it as a demonstration of what his disciples were to do. As he loved them and gave his life for them, the disciples were to do the same.

But imitation means more than imitating his actions. It refers to purpose and mission. As the Father sent him into the world, he is sending us into the world. He is the light of the world. We are to be the light of the world. Jesus' mission of seeking and saving the lost and of bringing the kingdom of heaven to earth is our mission.

Paul said, "Imitate me as I imitate Christ." You can understand that in two ways. The most common is to understand that if we imitate Paul, we will wind up imitating Jesus. The second, is that we should imitate Jesus, looking to Paul as an example. That, I think, is the better understanding. Any disciple of Jesus should be able to say to another, "Imitate Jesus as I imitate him."

When we look at the gospel of John, we see that Jesus was perfectly modeling God the Father to the world. In John 12:45, Jesus says of himself, that whoever has seen him has seen the one who sent him. If we become disciples of Jesus, we are becoming through Jesus, the disciples of the one who sent Jesus. That is, we take on the mission and works of God, as modeled by Jesus. This means that seeking and saving the lost, and bringing the kingdom of heaven to earth, becomes the mission of our lives. Jesus said, "As the Father has sent me, even so I am sending you, John 14:21b.

Makes disciples using their rabbi's teachings:

In the latter part of the first chapter of John, we have the example of the first five disciples to follow Jesus. Two were sent, two were called by the other disciples, and one was called by Jesus. Two of them participated in making other disciples; they were "disciple-makers." But it was Jesus who discipled them all.

Reading progressively through this list of five practices, you should realize that the natural work of a disciple is to make other disciples. Once you begin a life as a disciple of Jesus, you will make other disciples. Disciples reproduce, fulfilling God is first commandment in Genesis 1:28, "Be fruitful, multiply, fill the earth, and subdue it." This is establishing the kingdom of God upon the earth.

Toward the end of Luke 14, Jesus says that to be his disciples we must set aside everything, and even our own lives. A soldier practices and trains. In combat, he must consider that what he is living and fighting for is worth dying for. The disciples of Jesus learned and practiced these disciplines. They also called him "Lord" and lived that way. They faithfully lived their lives to make disciples and, save John, they all died violent deaths for him.

Jesus said, "Make disciples." Unless we understand what, a disciple is, we are unlikely to make one. Understanding what a disciple is requires more than just information; we need to be one ourselves. Jesus modeled being a disciple of his Father. Paul clearly stated that he himself modeled what it meant to be a disciple of Jesus. We should each be able to make the same claim.

6. Is there a difference between a believer, a follower, and a disciple?

Exploring the dynamics between Jesus and those he sent, as is presented in Matthew 28:16-20, should help us understand Matthew's choice of words for identifying those to whom Jesus gave his final command. What is commonly referred to as the Great Commission is not sending us off to make disciples on our own; rather it is the instructions for disciples to continue to work with Jesus in an ongoing "Great Partnership."

First, look at the grammar in the koine Greek. The word usually translated as "**go**" and make disciples, is actually "**having gone**" make disciples. Making disciples is not a journey or another "task," but it is what disciples were to do all the time, everywhere. Disciple-making is the lifestyle that Jesus left them. Bringing the kingdom that is in heaven to earth is the mission. (There are other verses where the disciples are told to "go," but this is not one of them.)

Secondly, look at the involvement of Jesus. He holds all the authority, and he will be with us until the end of the age. In other words, disciple-making is an intimate partnership involving Jesus and his disciples. Jesus did not "launch" his disciples into the world. He established a working relationship with them through the Holy Spirit.

This brings us to look at the distinctions between the different terms for saints.

What is a believer and how are they to be involved in the Great Commission? In John 3:16, we see that those who believe in Jesus will have eternal life. However, when we look at John 2:23-25 we see that Jesus would not entrust himself to believers. If you understand the Great Commission as a partnership with Jesus, then the element of trust and entrusting is fundamental.

> *Believers call Jesus, "Savior." Their prayer tends to be 'bless me' types of prayers. The focus is Salvation.*

If you want to mobilize "believers" to the Great Commission, you will fail. Jesus will not work with them. If your goal is to have people believe in Jesus, and you see that as the Great Commission, you will not see the importance of equipping them to replicate and multiply.

So, how does that impact your work to equip the saints or be equipped yourself, for the work of the ministry? What should you do or change?

What is a follower and how are they involved in the Great Commission? In Matthew 4 we see that Jesus calls four men to follow him. He adds, "And I will make you fishers of men." So, becoming a follower is an essential step in becoming a disciple. Followers are in the process of transformation. They are in the discipling process. The goal, however, is to become fishers of men. It is externally oriented, not on self-improvement.

Followers see their rabbi as their teacher. He is a person who will give them something or deepen their understanding of God. But are "followers" people to whom Jesus will fully entrust himself?

In Luke 14:25-26, Jesus addresses a large group of people who are following him and says unless they hate those closest to them and even their own lives and carry their own crosses, they cannot be his disciples. Jesus is looking for something much more than people who see him as a great teacher or someone who can do things for them.

As was mentioned earlier, it is interesting that in Matthew's account of Jesus foretelling that one of the disciples would betray him, that all the disciples became sad and one after another said, "<u>Lord</u> is it I?." Judas Iscariot, however, asks, rabbi – (<u>teacher</u>) is it I?" The difference between Jesus as your Lord and Jesus as a great teacher involves who you are willing to both live for and die for.

> *Followers call Jesus, "Teacher." Their prayer tends to be 'change me' types of prayer. The focus is Sanctification.*

What is a Disciple – The disciple that Jesus is looking for is first and foremost, trustworthy. We have already looked at the five defining practices of a disciple, but the final question is who the disciple is willing to give his life for.

> *Disciples call Jesus, "Lord." Their prayer tends to be 'use me' types of prayers. The focus is on the Great Commission.*

Looking at Matthew 28:16 and just reading the text, it is disciples who receive, and are capable of fulfilling the Great Commission. If you want to be involved in the Great Commission, you need to become a disciple of Jesus. Look at the five practices and do a personal inventory, then look at ways to strengthen the weak areas.

The best tool to do that is the Discovery Bible Study, which I will describe shortly.

7. What is the work of ministry that every saint is to be equipped to do and how is that done?

The goal of this book is to help move the traditional Church from the restrictive funnel in the first illustration to an inverted funnel which symbolizes what the early church experienced. This same model is happening around the world in disciple-making and in church-planting movements. I believe applying what you learn from the Bible to fulfill Ephesians 4:11 and 12 is key to helping the Church transition into a model that will reach everyone in the world. Refocusing on making disciples rather than converts is the motor that will generate the needed changes. Understanding the work of ministry to be all the ministry of Jesus, will give direction to bringing God's kingdom to earth and equipping the Church to bring down the gates of Hell.

8. **What is the difference between modern-day discipleship and disciple-making?** Is it possible to be discipled by Jesus? –

In modern <u>discipleship</u>, a mature Christian will disciple an immature one. It is usually one-on-one, but sometimes one person disciples a group. The discipler directs the disciple to look at Jesus and teaches, trains, and/or coaches them to maturity. By imitating the discipler, the disciple has a tangible model for spiritual and personal growth. The result is an increase in maturity and an expansion in understanding and potential they can grow into.

<u>Disciple-making</u> differs from discipling in that Jesus via the Holy Spirit directly does the discipling. The disciple is taught directly from the Bible under the tutelage of the Holy Spirit. The disciple is accountable to memorize and share the scripture with others, and to obey what the Holy Spirit reveals to him or her through it. All of this is based on the following scriptures.

In Matthew 18:20 we are promised that whenever two or three are gathered in his name, he is present. In John 1:1, we are told that the "word is God." In John 14:26, Jesus promised us that the Holy Spirit would teach us all things. In Matthew 23:8-11, Jesus tells us that each disciple is a brother and servant to one another, while Jesus is the teacher. The focus on and obedience to the scripture under the tutelage of the Holy Spirit, and mutual accountability. These are the keys to the success of the process of scripture-based disciple-making.

The advantage to this type of disciple-making is that once the process is learned and followed, any person may facilitate the disciple-making process. Just as Andrew invited his brother Simon, and Philip invited Nathaniel, so any disciple can invite another to become a disciple of Jesus. This lends itself to rapid multiplication. Obedience to the Scripture leads to rapid maturity and spiritual growth. Jesus and the Holy Spirit through the scriptures, can mature each disciple to their greatest potential. The disciples learn directly from the scripture without the imposition of a foreign culture. As Paul did, modeling by a disciple-maker is still important, but it is Jesus himself, who does the discipling.

9. Considering what you understand about Jesus, what is your purpose and goal for your life?

If you are serious about your relationship with Jesus, this is the most important personal question you can ask yourself.

For many people just being assured of the forgiveness of their sins and eternal salvation is all they have an interest in. But if they continue to listen to and read God's words, they will develop a deeper hunger to follow and conform their life to what they understand from the Bible. But this is all focused on the self. Jesus did not focus on himself. Neither did his disciples.

Much of the orientation of Christian work is focused on meeting the needs of the individual. There is forgiveness of sins, eternal destination, conforming our lives to that of Jesus. They are all legitimate needs and desires. However, living as a disciple has a different purpose than any of these. It is focused on completing the work that the Father gave to Jesus. The good news that Jesus brought is the kingdom of God. To establish that he came to seek and save the lost. Our personal salvation is essential to accomplish the goal of Jesus, but it is not the goal itself. Our sanctification is important, but it is not the goal.

If you take some time to think about what drew the disciples to Jesus, it was the desire to see the kingdom of God established in Israel. Only later, painfully later, did they understand that Jesus came to bring the kingdom of heaven to the whole earth. To be a disciple of Jesus is to be externally focused. It is to focus on glorifying God and bringing his kingdom to earth. To do this we must seek and save the lost; we must make disciples. It is externally focused, **not** focused on ourselves.

The first commandment God gave man was "Be fruitful, multiply, fill the earth, and subdue it." (Genesis 1:28) The Great Commission or Great Partnership is about doing that. From the beginning, God has given mankind a goal that is bigger than ourselves.

To Summarize:

I started this chapter by pointing out that my opinions are meant to give you a different perspective to consider. ("As iron sharpens iron so one man sharpens another," Proverbs 27:17) The purpose of sharing my understanding is that you have an opportunity to look at scriptures from a different perspective. This is not a "right" versus "wrong" presentation. If any of what I have written causes you to reflect and move into closer alignment with the words of the Bible, the purpose is served.

So how can we become disciples of Jesus and help others do the same? Let us close by looking at a process to do this.

A Discovery Bible Study is probably the best tool or process to accomplish all the five practices of a disciple. It has three basic parts.

- The first part is reflective and for reporting what God has done in your life. It includes thanksgiving and sharing your challenges. Then comes friendly accountability and testimony of how God has worked in your obedience.

- The second part is the study and memorization of some of God's word for understanding, both to obey and to tell others. After learning the passage well enough to retell, there are three basic questions to answer:
  - What is the story about?
  - What do we learn about people?
  - What do we learn about God or Jesus?
- The third part is application. How has our understanding changed and
  - What will we apply to our lives? "I will . . .."
  - Who will we tell what we have learned?
  - Who will we help?

There are many sources to learn about the discovery process; the following is a partial list which was current in 2024:

https://worldmissionsevangelism.com/resources
https://www.dbsguide.org/
https://www.contagiousdisciplemaking.com/
https://discoverapp.org/discovery-bible-study
https://discipleship.org/blog/
https://zume.training/resources/
Waha Discovery App https://tinyurl.com/33yymmtp

Conclusions

We began by considering the effectiveness of the Church in completing the Great Commission. We compared it to the picture of the church in the Acts of the Apostles. I have tried to show that one of the unaddressed barriers to completing the mission that Jesus has left us is our own thinking and its misalignment with the Bible, particularly the gospels.

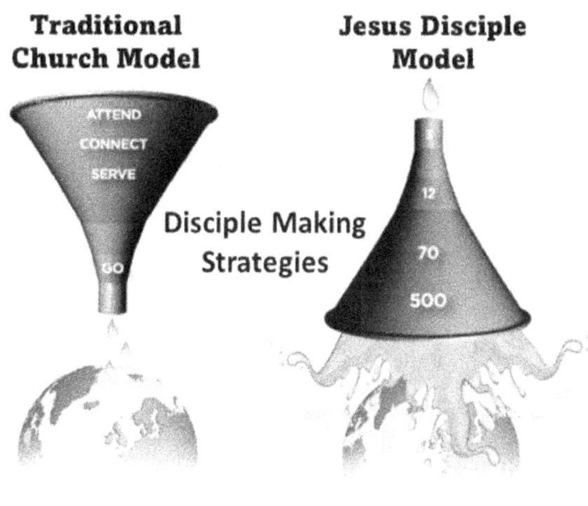

In Genesis 2, God tells Adam not to eat from the Tree of Knowledge of good and evil. In chapter 3, when the serpent challenges Eve, she says that God told them not to eat, <u>or even touch</u>, the fruit of the tree. Jesus chastised the Pharisees for adding rules and laws to the law of God, to the point that they negated the intent of God. In both these cases, the addition of man's rules and cautions to those of God produced unfruitfulness. The solution was and is, to go back to the words of God themselves.

I have shared my understanding, which is based upon reading the scripture and the testimony of a revitalized church where millions of people are being reached and discipled to Jesus. This corroboration gives me the confidence to speak and put this in writing.

If my understanding is helpful to you, I will be pleased. However, my understanding and opinions are not the important thing. The goal before us is to see the Church unencumbered by the restraints that it has placed on itself. Constraints not only of processes, policies, and practices, but also constraints on our minds.

In our current world, there are still billions of people who have not heard the gospel of Jesus. Yes, and the lands that were once called "Christian" are increasingly rejecting the Church and her Christ in their midst. If you are stirred to examine yourself, your assumptions, what you have **been** taught, and what you **have** taught, in light of the scriptures, particularly of the gospels, this little book has been a successful beginning point.

There are three goals I hope you set in your mind:

1. Become a disciple of Jesus.
2. Help others become his disciples and do the same.
3. Bring the kingdom of God to earth.

Jesus said if we abide in him and his word abides in us, we will bear much fruit. As in the diagram, may the word of God flow through us to our neighbors and into the world.

www.ingramcontent.com/pod-product-compliance
Lightning Source LLC
Chambersburg PA
CBHW072051150726
47996CB00015B/2478